Critter Favorites

Breakfast

Baboon Monkey Bread
Elephant Easy Eleganté
Egg Squares
Zebra's Zip Lock Omelet

Lunch

Lion's I'm Not Lyin' Pizza
Tortoise Tortilla Pie
Giraffe's Long Neck
Cheeseburgers

Snacks

Aardvark's No Bake Bark Bars
Gnu Canoes
Wild Dog Hot Dog Bites

Dinner

Gorilla La Lasagna
Hippopotamus' Hippo-Pot-A-Roast
Meerkat Messy Ribs
Cheetah's Cheesy Cheesy Chicken

Dessert

Crocodile Cranberry Pie
Wildebeest Wild Berry Crispy Crunch

Stuff You Will Need

Kitchen shears/scissors
Colander
2 and 4-cup glass
  measuring cups
Set of measuring spoons
Glass mixing bowls
Timer
6 quart slow cooker
12-cup mini muffin pan

Baking sheet pan
Rubber spatula
Potholders
Wax paper, aluminum foil,
  plastic wrap
Medium sized pot
Tongs
Large medal or wood spoon

Baboon – Monkey Bread

You need:

Cooking spray
Tube or bundt pan
Measuring cups
Measuring spoons

1 cup white sugar
2 teaspoons ground cinnamon

½ cup butter or margarine,
  1 stick
1 cup brown sugar

½ cup chopped peanuts or
  pecans
½ cup raisins, only if you like
  them

3 – 12 ounce packages,
refrigerated biscuit dough,
  (like Pillsbury Grands)

Directions: Heat oven to 350 degrees.

Spray your pan (not the kind with a removable bottom).

Mix sugar and cinnamon in a plastic bag, close tight and shake it up.

Take biscuits out of packages and with kitchen scissors cut each biscuit into 4 same size pieces (hint: cut in half, then cut halves in half). Shake the pieces in the sugar and cinnamon bag a few at a time.

Starting at the bottom of your pan, place the sugary pieces of dough in the pan until you build them up in a pile. Don't squish them down. As you build the pile, add some nuts and raisins here and there, if you want.

In a small bowl, place the butter or margarine and brown sugar in the microwave for about 1 minute until it's melted. (If you have a glass 4-cup measure, it's perfect for the microwave melting and pouring.) Using potholders carefully remove, stir and pour the mixture over the biscuit pile.

Bake for 35 minutes then remove very carefully using potholders. Let the pan cool for 10 minutes, no cheating. Using the potholders, turn the pan upside down on a big plate, let the sticky drip a few seconds upside down.

Woo hoo, ready to pull the sticky pieces apart, bite into and smile sticky smiles.

Elephant Easy
Eleganté Egg Squares

You need:

8" x 8" pan
Measuring cup
Medium bowl
Cooking spray
Timer
Fork

1-4 ounce can diced green chilis
   (These are NOT spicy)
2 cups grated Monterey Jack cheese
3 eggs

Directions: Spray the 8" X 8" pan. Turn oven to 350 degrees.

Crack eggs into medium bowl. Remove shells with your very clean fingers. Using a fork, break the yolks and stir up the eggs pretty well.

Add chilis and cheese. Mix well.

Pour into sprayed pan and bake until light brown. Set timer for 20 minutes.

When time is up and top is turning light brown, with potholders, remove the pan. Turn off the oven.

Cut the Eleganté Egg dish into squares. (Hint: Cut down the middle, then cut down the middle of the middles. Turn the pan and repeat.) You should have 16 squares.

Best breakfast ever that you can eat with your fingers!

This is also a great afternoon snack.

Zebra's Zip Lock Omelet

You need:
   (this makes 1 omelet)

1 quart-size freezer
   zip lock bag
Small bowl
Medium pot to boil water
Tongs

2 eggs

Any of the following:
Shredded cheddar cheese
Chopped cooked ham
Chopped green onion
Cooked bacon crumbles
Chopped mushrooms
Chopped red or green
pepper
Salsa
Hash brown potatoes

Directions: Fill a medium-sized pot 2/3 full with water and put it on the stove high heat to boil. After you get it boiling, turn the heat down so it bubbles but doesn't splatter water all over.

In a small bowl, crack open 2 eggs. Remove any shells. Open your zip lock bag and pour in the eggs. Seal the bag very tightly and using the outside of the bag, squish the eggs to break the yolk and make them scrambly. Doesn't take much squishing.

Make sure your hands are very clean. In the same small bowl put a small amount of any ingredients you like. (For example, a little cheese, a little bacon, a small amount of salsa, maybe some onion.)

After collecting your favorites, carefully open the zip lock bag with the egg in it and dump in your favorite ingredients. (This is easier if you set the bag in an empty bowl to hold it.) Get as much air out of the bag as possible and seal the bag very tightly without spilling the contents.

Place the bag very gently into the boiling water and set the timer for 13 minutes. When time is up, turn off the heat. Using tongs, remove the bag from the water, carefully open the bag and let the Zebra omelet roll out onto your plate. You can cook up to 6 bags at one time (put names on the bags).

Lion – I'm Not Lyin' Pizza

You need:

Large baking sheet pan
Measuring cup
Measuring spoons
Ruler
Metal spatula

1 package refrigerated
biscuits – big, flaky kind

1 cup pizza sauce from jar

2 cups shredded mozzarella cheese
1 small package sliced pepperoni
Other stuff: olives, mushrooms,
     peppers, cooked sausage, ham

Directions: Turn the oven to 375 degrees.

With clean hands, one at a time, place a biscuit on the baking pan and using your very clean fingers smash it down to make a circle about 6 inches across (use a ruler or not, it doesn't have to be perfect).

After all the biscuits are on the pan, cover each biscuit with 2 Tablespoons of pizza sauce, ¼ cup mozzarella cheese and as many slices of pepperoni you want or can fit.

Set the timer and bake in the oven for 15 minutes.

Yikes, very hot! When time is up, remove pan using potholders. Place each pizza on a plate using a metal spatula or pie server.

This is a great pizza and we're not lyin'.

Remember to turn off the oven.

Tortoise Tortilla Pie

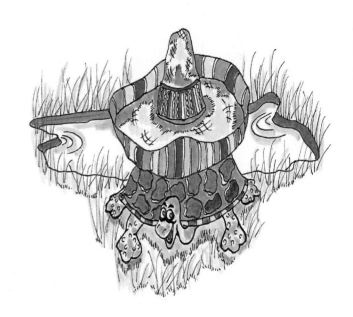

You need:

Deep dish pie plate
Cooking spray
Measuring cup
Large bowl and small bowl
Measuring spoons
Colander for draining beans
Aluminum foil
Potholder
Timer

2-15 ounce cans pinto beans, drained and rinsed
¾ cup salsa
½ teaspoon garlic powder

¼ cup salsa
2 tablespoons fresh cilantro, chopped (optional)
1-15 ounce can black beans, drained and rinsed
½ cup chopped tomatoes, squeeze out juice

7-8" flour tortillas

2 cups shredded cheddar cheese

***Directions*:** Turn on oven to 400 degrees.

With very clean hands, dump the pinto beans into a large bowl and smoosh (mash) the beans with your hands or a fork. After they're smooshed, add the salsa and garlic. Mix well. This bowl should have all the green ingredients.

In a small bowl, mix together all the red ingredients.

Spray the deep dish pie plate with cooking spray. Place 1 tortilla on the bottom of the plate and spread ¾ cup of pinto bean mixture over the tortilla but not all the way to the edge. Top with ¼ cup cheese.

Place another tortilla on top and spread 2/3 cup black bean mixture (red ingredients in the small bowl) nearly to the edge. Top with ¼ cup cheese.

Repeat this 3 more times. Tortilla, pinto mixture, cheese, tortilla, black bean mixture, cheese, etc. (Ending with pinto mixture and cheese.) Press down on the top a bit and cover with aluminum foil. Set the timer for 45 minutes and bake.

Turn off oven. Remove the pie from the oven very carefully using potholders. Cut into wedges like a pie to serve. (Note: the bottom tortilla sometimes remains in the pie plate.)

Giraffe – Long Neck Cheeseburgers

You need:

Large baking sheet pan
Cooking spray
Aluminum foil
Rubber spatula
Potholders
Large bowl
Measuring cups and spoons
Timer

1 pound lean ground beef
1 teaspoon salt
¼ teaspoon pepper
1 tablespoon Worcestershire
   sauce
¼ cup catsup
1 tablespoon dried grated
   onion
½ cup oatmeal (not instant)
½ cup milk

3 large hot dog buns, sliced
open

1 cup shredded cheddar
cheese

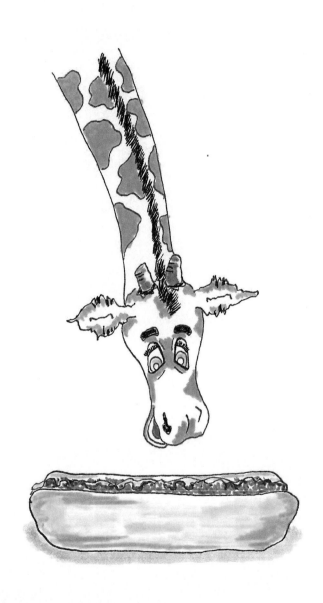

Directions: Turn on oven to 350 degrees. Spray the baking sheet pan. (This helps hold the aluminum foil on the pan.)

Put aluminum foil on the baking sheet, then spray again. Place each half of hot dog buns crust side down on the sprayed baking sheet (6 total).

Wash your hands really well. Then in a large bowl with your very clean hands, moosh together the ground beef and everything green. Using your fingers, spread the beef mixture all over the top (cut side) of the buns all the way to the edges. Pile it a little.

Set the timer and bake in the oven about 25 minutes. When time is complete, using potholders, carefully remove from the oven and top each baked beef mixture with the shredded cheese. With potholders, return the pan to the oven and bake 5 more minutes.

Very hot! Remember potholders, remove the baking sheet from the oven and using a spatula, place each cheeseburger on individual plates.

So good!

Aardvark No Bake Bark Bars

You need:

Cooking spray
Glass bowl
Measuring cups
Measuring spoons
Large metal or
   wooden spoon
12-cup muffin pan
Potholders

2 cups miniature marshmallows
2 tablespoons unsalted butter
1 tablespoon unsweetened cocoa
1/4 teaspoon vanilla extract
1/8 teaspoon salt

3 cups whole-grain cereal
   (such as Cheerios, Kashi Go
   Lean, Kix, Wheaties, Grape Nuts)

1/2 cup semisweet chocolate chips

Directions: Spray your muffin pan with cooking spray. Be sure to coat each cup.

Combine marshmallows, butter, cocoa, vanilla, and salt in a large microwave-safe glass bowl. Microwave on HIGH for 1 minute. Using potholders, very carefully remove bowl from microwave.

Coat a large metal or wooden spoon with cooking spray. (This is important because it helps to stir sticky stuff.) Hold the bowl with a potholder since the bowl may be hot. With the coated spoon, stir the stuff in the bowl. Be strong. This isn't easy. Be sure to scrape up the melty, sticky stuff on the bottom. All the marshmallows should be melted. If not, you may have to microwave another 10 seconds. Mix well.

Stir in cereal until all of it is coated with sticky stuff. Stir in chocolate chips.

Coat a 1/4-cup measuring cup with cooking spray to use as a scoop. Using your very clean fingers lightly pack measuring cup with cereal mixture. Scoop out of the measuring cup and moosh into the muffin pan. One per cup to end up with 12 bars. You can pat each one down a little if you want. Freeze 8 minutes or until firm.

Remove from freezer – enjoy varky barky balls. Store in refrigerator.

Gnu Canoes

You need:

Measuring cup
Measuring spoons
Medium mixing bowl
Kitchen shears
Plate

1 cup Miracle Whip
1-4 ounce jar diced pimiento,
    drained
1 teaspoon Worcestershire
    sauce
1 teaspoon grated dried onion
1/4 teaspoon ground red pepper
    (optional)

12 oz finely shredded sharp
    cheddar cheese

6 celery sticks, cut into 4-inch pieces

Stir together Miracle Whip and rest of red ingredient in a medium bowl. Mix well.

Stir in cheese a little at a time until all mixed.

Using very clean fingers, pile and stuff the cheese mixture into each celery stick. Place on plate, cheese side up.

The best snack ever!

If you have cheese mixture left over, store in refrigerator for tomorrow. Yay!

Wild Dog (African) – Hot Dog Bites

You need:

12-cup mini muffin pan
Cooking spray
Measuring cups
Measuring spoons
Medium bowl

3 hot dogs

1 box Jiffy cornbread
   mix
¼ cup milk
1 egg
1 tablespoon honey
¼ cup shredded
   cheddar

Directions:

Turn oven to 375 degrees.

Spray the mini muffin pan and Tablespoon measure with cooking spray. (Note: honey will slide off sprayed Tablespoon.)

Make the cornbread. In a medium bowl, beat the egg a little bit with a fork, then add in honey, cheese and milk. Mix. Dump in the dry stuff from the Jiffy box. With a large spoon, stir only until all the dry stuff is wet. Shouldn't stir much.

Cut each hot dog into 4 equal pieces with kitchen scissors. (Easy way – cut hot dog in half, then cut the halves in half.)

With teaspoon, fill each muffin cup ½ full with cornbread mixture. Then stand one hot dog piece in the center of the batter.

Place in oven and bake for 10 minutes. Using potholders, carefully remove from the oven and let cool 5 minutes before removing from the pan. Turn off the oven.

The best dog bites ever!

Gorilla LaLa Lasagna

You need:

5-6 quart slow cooker
Cooking spray
Medium bowl
Measuring cup
Clean kitchen towel
Timer
Teaspoon

1-26 ounce jar marinara sauce
1-14 ½ ounce can of diced tomatoes with
   basil, garlic, oregano
1-8 ounce package of no-boil lasagna noodles
1-15 ounce container of part-skim ricotta cheese
1-8 ounce shredded mozzarella cheese

1-10 ounce frozen chopped spinach, thawed

Directions:

Spray the inside of the slow cooker really well.

Place thawed spinach in a clean kitchen towel, twist it and squeeze as hard as you can over the kitchen sink to get out all the liquid. Divide into 4 piles.

In the bowl, combine the marinara sauce and the diced tomatoes. Stir up.

Measure 1 cup of the marinara/tomato mixture and spread it around the bottom of the slow cooker.

Place 4 noodles over the sauce (OK to overlap). With teaspoon drop about ½ cup ricotta cheese on the noodles (OK to spread around with very clean fingers) and top with ½ cup of the mozzarella cheese. Add 1/4 of the spinach.

Repeat the layers. One cup marinara/tomato mixture, 4 noodles, ½ cup ricotta, ½ cup mozzarella, 1/4 of spinach. Repeat two more times, ending with what's left of marinara/tomato mixture.

Cover the slow cooker and set on LOW. Set the timer for 3 hours. Turn off the slow cooker and scoop out the yumminess.

Meerkat Messy Ribs

You need:

5-6 quart slow cooker or larger
Measuring cups
Measuring spoons

1 large onion, sliced thickly
1 cup katsup
¼ cup vinegar, apple cider or
   red wine
3 tablespoons brown sugar
2 tablespoons flour

1 teaspoon salt
1 teaspoon paprika
1 teaspoon curry
½ teaspoon dry mustard
½ teaspoon chili powder
10 ounce can beef consomme

3 pounds country style pork ribs

Directions: Set the slow cooker on HIGH.

In a medium saucepan, add all the red ingredients. Cook and stir over medium heat until everything is combined and looks like a messy, sticky mixture. No need to boil.

Place ribs in bottom of slow cooker. Pour the messy mixture over the ribs.

Cover the slow cooker, set it on HIGH then set a timer for 1 hour. At the end of the hour, turn the cooker setting to LOW and set the timer for 7 hours.

When complete, turn off the slow cooker, carefully remove the lid.

Remove the ribs with a slotted spoon and scoop the messy, sticky, yummy sauce into a separate bowl to serve with the ribs.

Meerkats LOVE this stuff!

Hippopotamus – Hippo Pot-a-Roast

You need:

6 Quart slow cooker (like
Crockpot)
Slotted spoon
Large bowl and plate for lid

2 pound beef chuck roast,
  no need to brown

1 can (14.5 ounce), low sodium
  beef broth
1 package dry vegetable soup

8 yukon or fingerling (little)
  potatoes, rinsed and dried
  a bit on paper towel, peels on
4 celery stalks, rinse well, then
  using scissors, cut off the
  bottom part, leave the top leafy
  part, cut stalks in big chunks
1 small bag peeled baby carrots
1 jar cocktail pearl onions, drain
  the juice

1 can cream of celery soup
1 package beef stew
  seasoning mix

Directions: In 4-cup glass measure, measure the beef broth, then add the dry vegetable soup. Stir well until the powdery soup bits disappear but the little veggie parts are OK.

Place the potatoes, celery, and carrots on the bottom of the slow cooker. Put the beef roast on top of vegetables. Dump in the pearl onions. Pour broth mixture over all.

Place the lid on the slow cooker and turn the setting to "HIGH". Set the timer for 1 hour. After one hour, move the setting to "LOW" and set the timer for 6 hours.

When the cooking is complete, very carefully (use a slotted spoon if you have one) remove the meat and vegetables and put them in a large bowl. Use a plate to make a lid for the bowl which helps keep everything warm. All the good juices are still in the slow cooker. Turn the setting to "HIGH".

In a small bowl, combine the can of celery soup and the package of beef stew seasoning. Stir really well. Pour the soup and seasoning mixture into the slow cooker and stir the good juices and the mixture together. Keep stirring until everything is mixed, then set the timer for 5 minutes and let it warm through.

To serve. Scoop out some meat and the vegetables that you have been keeping warm onto a plate. Spoon some gravy from the slow cooker over the meat and veggies.

Ready to devour. Hip hippo hooray!

Cheetah - Cheesy Cheesy Chicken

You need:

Cooking spray
3 mixing bowls
Small baking sheet
Potholders

½ cup flour
1 teaspoon salt
1 teaspoon pepper
1 teaspoon garlic powder
1 egg
1 tablespoon milk
1 cup shredded cheddar cheese
½ cup Italian seasoned bread
  crumbs
1 cup crispy cereal, like
  Rice Krispies

4 skinless, boneless chicken
  breasts
2 tablespoons butter, melted

Directions:

Heat oven to 350 degrees. Spray small baking sheet pan.

Prepare 3 bowls:
#1 bowl – mix flour, salt, pepper, garlic powder
#2 bowl – beat together egg and milk
#3 bowl – mix cheese, cereal, bread crumbs

Put the bowls in this order – 1, 2, 3

Pat chicken pieces with a paper towel to dry a little. With very clean fingers,
roll a chicken piece in #1 bowl, then in #2, then press on mixture in #3. Place on sprayed baking sheet pan. Do this for each chicken piece.

Super wash your hands with soap and water.

Microwave the butter in a glass measuring cup. Remove from the microwave
using potholders. Drizzle chicken with melted butter and bake in the oven for
about 30 – 40 minutes. Should be golden brown.

Yummy, cheesy cheetah cheery chicken.

Crocodile Crazy Cranberry Pie

You need:

1 mixing bowl
Plastic wrap

1-14 1/2 ounce can whole berry cranberry sauce

1-8 ounce tub of whipped topping, like Cool Whip, thawed

1-8 ounce package of cream cheese, left 30 minutes at
   room temperature

 1-ready made graham cracker crust

Directions:

This is very important. Put the cream cheese on the kitchen counter for at least 30 minutes before you begin. Cream cheese should be room temperature, not cold, otherwise it will be hard to stir.

In a large mixing bowl, pour in cranberries, whipped topping and cream cheese. Mix well, but gently so you don't moosh down the whipped topping too much. Fluffy is good.

Pour the mixture into the pie crust.

Loosely cover with plastic wrap and place in the freezer for 1 hour.

Yum! Crocs are crazy for this stuff!

Hint: After first servings, keep the pie in the freezer but set it out on the kitchen counter about 15 minutes before you're ready to eat. Much easier to slice when it's thawed a bit and very much tastier.

Wildebeest Wild Berry Crispy Crunch

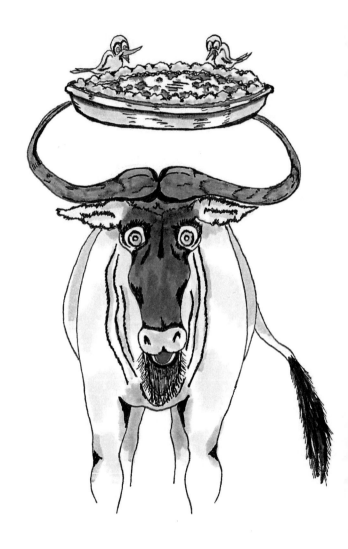

You need:

Cooking spray
2 mixing bowls
9" pie plate
Potholders
Measuring spoons
Timer

2-12 oz. Packages
   frozen mixed berries
¾ cup flour
¼ cup white sugar
1 tablespoon lemon juice

3/4 cup oatmeal, not instant
2/3 cup brown sugar
1 teaspoon cinnamon
½ teaspoon ground ginger
¼ teaspoon ground nutmeg

7 tablespoons cold unsalted butter

Directions:

Heat oven to 375 degrees.

Spray pie plate.

In medium bowl, dump in frozen berries, white sugar, and flour. Mix well and add to pie plate.

In another bowl, mix together all of orange ingredients, except butter. Break up butter in small pieces. With very clean hands, add the butter pieces to the orange ingredients and moosh until most of orange ingredients are held together with butter (should be clumpy).

Sprinkle clumpy mixture over the top of the berries and carefully place in the oven.

Set the oven timer for 1 hour. When done, remove very carefully using potholders. Turn off the oven. Let the Crispy Crunch rest for 15 minutes before serving. Your choice – serve it warm or at room temperature.

Note: Many wildebeests like this with vanilla ice cream on top.

Happy Critter Cooking

- Kai Brown, Author
- Doug McLeod, Illustrator

48798783R00021

Made in the USA
San Bernardino, CA
05 May 2017